X 972.92 G796
35250001185255
89ynf
Green, Jen.
Jamaica

P9-CAA-878

10/09

EUROPE

A S I A

Pacific

Ocean

AFRICA

A

Indian

Ocean

AUSTRALIA

ANTARCTICA

THIS BOOK PURCHASED THROUGH
THE GENEROUS BEQUEST OF
GLORIA AUERMILLER

Jamaica

Jen Green

David J. Howard and Joel Frater, Consultants

NATIONAL GEOGRAPHIC

WASHINGTON, D.C.

WWW.SHOREWOODLIBRARY.ORG

Contents

Foreword

Jamaica is a great place to relax and enjoy a rich heritage and culture. The island lies in the Caribbean Sea about 600 miles (965 km) south of Miami, Florida. Jamaica's landscape ranges from rolling hills rich with lush vegetation to coastal plains that taper into breathtaking beaches. The hills and plains are ideal for agriculture, while the coastal areas feature many resorts that support the country's leading industry, tourism.

Jamaica offers a combination of two worlds. The first is highly Westernized and developed. It can be seen in the island's tourism and mining industries or in cities like Kingston, the capital, and Montego Bay. Chief among the industries is bauxite, from which aluminum is made. The second Jamaica is a rural place, where families raise just enough food to eat on small farms. The customs of rural communities are steeped in tradition, as is clear from revivalist church services and funerals, popular games such as dominoes and cricket, and family gatherings.

Much of what is unique about Jamaica is summed up in the island's motto—"Out of Many, One People"—or in the symbolism of the black, green, and gold flag. Black stands for hardships overcome and to be faced; gold, for natural wealth and beauty of sunlight; and green stands for hope and agricultural resources. Despite the legacies of colonialism and slavery, Jamaicans have been able to harness a shared spirit that has brought together people of various ethnic origins for nation building. Their laid-back attitude, friendly smile, and unique expressions, such as "no problem mon" or "irie mon," create a magnetism that is irresistible.

Jamaica's government is confronted with many social challenges, including high levels of crime and pressure on the provision of health care

and education, yet its people continue to be resilient and remain eager to seek opportunities for self-improvement and to maintain a sense of national pride.

This book provides a bird's-eye view of Jamaica by showing readers its fascinating geography and nature, its history and struggles for independence, its people and culture, and its government and economy. In 2008, Jamaica celebrated its 46th year of independence. It will be fascinating to follow the journey of this tiny yet proud nation as it charts its course for the next 46 years.

▲ **A luxury liner is docked in the bay at Ochio Ríos, a busy city on the north coast of Jamaica.**

Joel Frater
State University of New York,
College at Brockport

An
Island
Paradise

XAYMACA, "LAND OF WOOD AND WATER"—
that is what Jamaica's original inhabitants, the
Taino people, called their island. Sure enough,
the mountainous Caribbean island is covered in
dense green forest and cut by hundreds of fast-flowing
streams. The water has carved deep ravines through
the hills and formed stepped cascades.

Christopher Columbus, the first European person
to set eyes on Jamaica, called it "the fairest island that
eyes have beheld." As well as forests and waterfalls,
Jamaica also has mist-covered mountains and fertile
valleys. For centuries these were the site of coffee and
sugar plantations, the source of the island's wealth.
Today the island is also known as a tourist destination,
thanks to mile upon mile of sandy beaches.

◀ Dunn's River Falls is a scenic area; people like to climb up the steps of rock.

WHAT'S THE WEATHER LIKE?

Lying 18° north of the equator, Jamaica has a hot, sunny climate. Temperatures vary little with the seasons, but the coasts are considerably warmer than the highlands. Temperatures here fall to just 50° F (10° C) in winter. On the coasts, the moist, sticky air is freshened by trade winds blowing off of the sea. Jamaicans know these welcome winds as the "Doctor Breeze." The island has two rainy seasons, one in early summer, the other in the fall. The coasts receive about 30 inches (76 cm) of rain, while 100 inches (510 cm) fall in the highlands. Hurricanes are common in late summer. The map opposite shows the physical features of Jamaica.

Labels on this map and similar maps throughout this book identify most of the places pictured in each chapter.

Fast Facts

OFFICIAL NAME: Jamaica

FORM OF GOVERNMENT: Parliamentary democracy

CAPITAL: Kingston

POPULATION: 2,780,132

OFFICIAL LANGUAGE: English

CURRENCY: Jamaican dollar

AREA: 4,411 square miles (10,992 square kilometers)

BORDERING NATIONS: None

HIGHEST POINT: Blue Mountain Peak, 7,402 feet (2,256 meters)

LOWEST POINT: Sea level, 0 feet (0 meters)

MAJOR MOUNTAIN RANGES: Blue Mountains, John Crow Mountains, Don Figuero Mountains, Cockpit Country

LONGEST RIVERS: Black River, Rio Cobre, Rio Grande

COASTLINE: 634 miles (1,022 kilometers)

Average Temperature & Rainfall

Average High/Low Temperatures; Yearly Rainfall

KINGSTON (SOUTH COAST): 88° F (31° C) / 77° F (25° C); 35 in (89 cm)

MONTEGO BAY (NORTH COAST): 86° F (30° C) / 75° F (24° C); 45 in (114 cm)

Jamaica Channel

Blue Mountains

Caribbean Sea

Caribbean Sea

0   mi   20

0   km   20

MAP KEY
Tropical
Tropical wet and dry

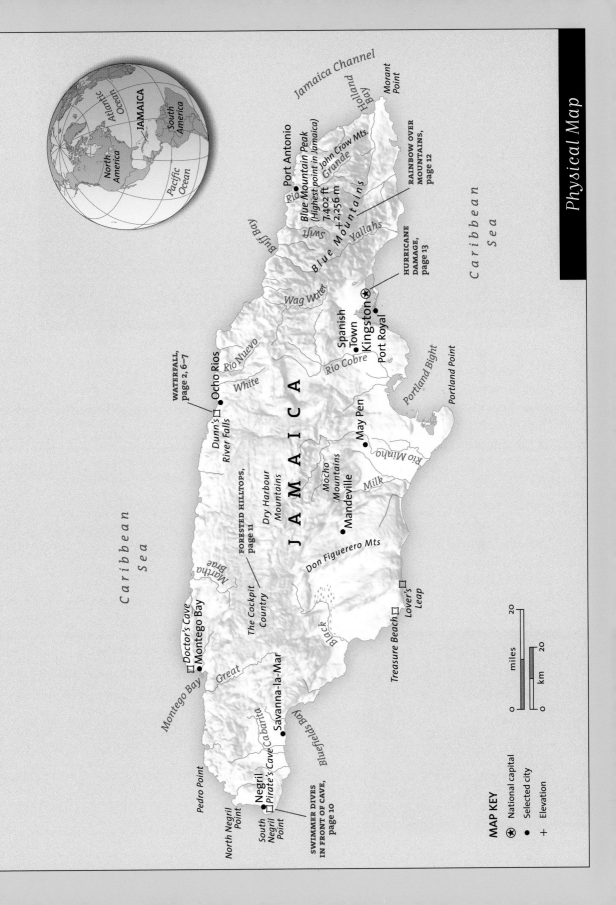

Physical Map

MAP KEY

⊛ National capital

● Selected city

+ Elevation

Caribbean Sea

Caribbean Sea

Jamaica Channel

JAMAICA

North America

Atlantic Ocean

JAMAICA

South America

Pacific Ocean

Pedro Point

North Negril Point

South Negril Point

Negril

Pirate's Cave

SWIMMER DIVES IN FRONT OF CAVE, page 10

Savanna-la-Mar

Bluefields Bay

Cabarita

Great

Montego Bay Point

Montego Bay

Doctor's Cave

Martha Brae

The Cockpit Country

FORESTED HILLTOPS, page 11

Dunn's River Falls

WATERFALL, page 2, 6–7

Ocho Rios

White

Rio Nuevo

Dry Harbour Mountains

Don Figuerero Mts

Black

Treasure Beach

Lover's Leap

Mocho Mountains

Mandeville

Milk

May Pen

Rio Minho

Rio Cobre

Spanish Town

Port Royal

Kingston

Portland Bight

Portland Point

Wag Water

Buff Bay

Swift

Yallahs

Blue Mountains

Blue Mountain Peak (Highest point in Jamaica) 7,402 ft + 2,256 m

John Crow Mts.

Grande

Rio

Port Antonio

Holland Bay

Morant Point

HURRICANE DAMAGE, page 13

RAINBOW OVER MOUNTAINS, page 12

J A M A I C A

miles   0   20

km   0   20

A man dives into the sea at Pirate's Cave in Negril. The remote coast provided bases for pirates during the 17th and 18th centuries.

An ancient tree on a rugged part of Jamaica's coast twists out above a rocky cliff edge.

Gem of the Caribbean

Jamaica is the third-largest island in the Caribbean. Covering 4,411 square miles (10,992 square km), it is about the same size as the U.S. state of Connecticut. With its long, squashed oval shape, it measures 146 miles (230 km) long and about 35 miles (55 km) wide.

Jamaica is part of a chain of large Caribbean islands called the Greater Antilles, along with Cuba, Hispaniola, and Puerto Rico. These islands are partly volcanic but were formed mainly by a collision between two of the immense plates that make up Earth's crust. When the North American and Caribbean plates slowly crashed together about 25 million years ago, the area between them was crumpled upward to form high ground that is now a chain of islands. Jamaica is really the tip of a huge mountain rising from the seafloor.

A NATURAL HIDEOUT

Cockpit Country (right) in the western highlands is a wild limestone landscape pitted with deep hollows known locally as "cockpits." There are also rocky crags, sheer gullies, and deep caves. The soft limestone rock has been eaten away by trickling water to form all of these features. This eroded landscape is called karst scenery.

Cockpit Country has few villages or roads. For many years it was used as a hiding place for runaway slaves known as the Maroons. British soldiers looking for the runaways would walk through the forest back-to-back to watch out for ambushers. For this reason, the region was called "The Land of Look Behind."

Rugged Landscapes

It is said that when the explorer Christopher Columbus was asked to describe Jamaica, he crumpled up a sheet of paper and tossed it on a table. Jamaica is a craggy mass of mountains and plateaus cut by deep valleys. Around half of the island stands more than 1,000 feet (330 m) above sea level.

A spine of mountains runs west to east across Jamaica. In the west is a high plateau pitted with deep hollows, called Cockpit Country. To the east lie the John Crow Mountains and the Blue Mountains, which contain the island's highest point, Blue Mountain Peak.

Coastal Strip

On some parts of Jamaica's coast, the mountains drop steeply to the sea, forming sheer cliffs, such as Lover's Leap on the south coast. However, most of the island's coast is a flat plain. The coastal plain forms a strip that

MOUNTAINS IN THE MIST

The Blue Mountains in the east are Jamaica's highest mountains. Moist winds blowing off the ocean form rain clouds there, making a blue misty haze that hangs over the uplands and gives them their name. Streams and rivers carry the rain down from the Blue Mountains to coastal cities, including Kingston. These rivers provide water for half of Jamaica's population. The mist also provides moisture for lush vegetation. Different plants grow at different heights up the mountains. Ferns, palms, and bamboos are found on the lower slopes. This is also the

▲ A rainbow and cloud hang over the Blue Mountains of Jamaica.

location of the plantations that grow the famous Blue Mountain coffee. Higher slopes are covered with small twisty trees, called elfin forest, while the peaks have only shrubs.

is only 12 miles (20 km) across at its widest points. Most of the island's towns and cities are found here, including the capital, Kingston. The coastal strip is also the location of much of the island's farming. These lowlands are a patchwork of fields and plantations where bananas, citrus fruits, and sugarcane are grown.

Water and Sand

Jamaica has more than 120 small rivers. The longest is the Black River. Its lower stretch is smooth enough for boats to travel up and down. However, most other rivers drop too steeply to be navigable. The island's coasts are dotted with beautiful beaches that attract thousands of tourists, forming the basis of one of

Jamaica's main industries. The beaches of the north and west are covered with fine white sand made from tiny pieces of shell. Parts of the southern coast have black volcanic sand. Some of the most beautiful beaches also have intriguing names: Bluefields Bay, Doctor's Cave, and Treasure Beach.

Natural Hazards

The first Europeans to see Jamaica compared it to the Garden of Eden. However, Jamaica's beautiful surroundings are always in danger of being ripped apart by natural disasters. The main risk comes from hurricanes. These enormous spinning storms blow in from the Atlantic between June and October, wreaking havoc with roaring winds and lashing rain. In 2004, Hurricane Ivan brought 165-mile-per-hour (265 km/h) winds that wrecked crops and ports. In 2007 Hurricane Dean gave the island another battering.

Earthquakes are also a hazard. In 1692 a severe earthquake destroyed the pirate city of Port Royal, while in 1907 a quake flattened most of Kingston.

▼ A fisher checks the damage caused to the shoreline of Kingston by Hurricane Dean in 2007.

A Haven for Birds

L IKE MANY CARIBBEAN ISLANDS, Jamaica is a bird spotter's heaven. Of 250 birds that can be seen on the island, 26 live nowhere else. These include the streamertail hummingbird. With its dark green, shimmering feathers and slender scarlet bill, this species is also known as the "doctor bird"—perhaps because its long tail feathers resemble the frock coat worn by doctors in the past.

The island also has the world's second-smallest bird, the tiny vervain, just 2.5 inches (8 cm) long. Another small resident is the tody. Its plumage of red, gold, and green—the colors of Jamaica's Rastafarian religion—earn it the nickname rasta bird. There are seabirds such as frigate birds. They are called pirates of the skies, because they steal food from other birds.

◀ A streamertail hummingbird—Jamaica's national bird—hovers beside a bleeding heart vine as it laps nectar from inside the flowers.

ISLAND WORLD

Jamaica holds so many habitats that it has been called "a world in one island." The map opposite shows the main vegetation zones—what grows where in Jamaica. Each zone is home to a distinct group of plants and animals. There are several types of forest, including lush coastal forest, elfin forests on mountainsides, and the dry forests of Cockpit Country. Cactus thrives in the dry grasslands on the south coast. Jamaica also has upland meadows and scrublands. Coastal habitats include mazes of cliffs, beaches, islands, and coral reefs. In the 1990s the Natural Resources Conservation Authority was set up to protect Jamaica's wildlife. The island now has three national parks: The Blue and John Crow Mountains Park and two marine parks at Negril Bay and Montego Bay. Several more parks are planned.

Species at Risk

Centuries of human settlement have created some problems for Jamaica's wildlife. Large areas of lowland forest have been cut down to provide timber or fuel, or to clear the way for towns, mines, or farms. Experts estimate that only about 7 percent of these lush forests remain. Animals such as the American crocodile, manatee, hutia, and iguana are now rare because so many have been killed for their meat and hides. New predators brought to the island by people, such as cats, dogs, and mongooses, have preyed on island creatures, while pigs and goats brought to provide meat have grazed some areas bare.

Species at risk include:

> American crocodile
> Black racer (lizard)
> Caribbean monk seal
> Hawksbill turtle
> Homerus swallowtail (butterfly)
> Jamaican boa (snake)
> Jamaican fig-eating bat
> Jamaican hutia (rodent)
> Jamaican iguana
> Loggerhead turtle
> West Indian manatee
> West Indian whistling duck

▼ Palm forest is protected in the Blue and John Crow Mountains National Park.

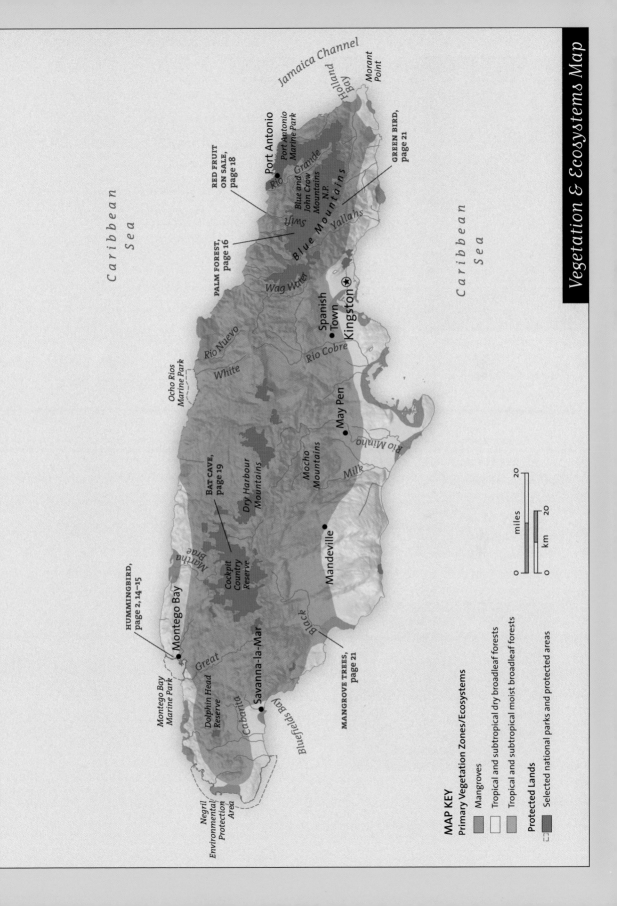

Vegetation & Ecosystems Map

Caribbean
Sea

Jamaica Channel

Morant
Point

Holland
Bay

Port Antonio
Marine Park

**RED FRUIT
ON SALE,**
page 18

Port Antonio

Rio

Blue and Grande

John Crow
Mountains
N.P.

GREEN BIRD,
page 21

Blue Mountains

Swift

Yallahs

PALM FOREST,
page 16

Wag Water

Rio Nuevo

Ocho Rios
Marine Park

Spanish
Town

⊛

Kingston

Rio Cobre

White

Caribbean
Sea

May Pen

Rio Minho

BAT CAVE,
page 19

Dry Harbour
Mountains

Mocho
Mountains

Milk

Mandeville

Martha
Brae

Cockpit
Country
Reserve

HUMMINGBIRD,
page 2, 14–15

Montego Bay

Black

Montego Bay
Marine Park

Great

Dolphin Head
Reserve

Savanna-la-Mar

Cabarita

MANGROVE TREES,
page 21

Bluefields Bay

Negril
Environmental
Protection
Area

MAP KEY

Primary Vegetation Zones/Ecosystems

- Mangroves
- Tropical and subtropical dry broadleaf forests
- Tropical and subtropical moist broadleaf forests

Protected Lands

- Selected national parks and protected areas

0   miles   20

0   km   20

Prolific Plants

Jamaica is famous for its vast range of plants. Of the 3,000 species growing there, more than a quarter are unique to the island. Scientists describe such species as "endemic." There are more than 200 orchids, with delicate flowers of all shapes and sizes. Jamaica has 550 different ferns and 60 bromeliads, which root high on the trunks of trees and so are nicknamed "air plants."

▲ A fruit seller shows off his stock of ackee, an African fruit used in Jamaican dishes.

▼ The colorful flowers of hibiscus are common in the Jamaican countryside, but they were only brought to the island by people in recent centuries.

Jamaica's forests, gardens, and hedges are bright with flowers such as spiky heliconia. Many flowers have been introduced by humans. In the same way, only guava, pineapple, and sweetsop are native Jamaican fruits. Sweetsop tastes like custard and is sometimes called the custard apple, even though the fruit is covered in green scales and does not look anything

like an apple. Bananas, breadfruit, coconut palms, and citrus trees were all brought either by Europeans or the Taino—the first inhabitants of the island. Ackee, a red-cased fruit used in Jamaica's national dish, saltfish and ackee, arrived with enslaved people from West Africa.

Palm trees such as royal palms and cabbage palms stand out among Jamaica's many trees. So do the silk cotton and the mahoe with its mottled trunk—the island's national tree. The delicate blue sprays of the *lignum vitae* are the national flower. This tree's name means "wood of life" because of the many medicines obtained from its bark.

Rabbit-Sized Rodents

Strolling through Jamaica's forests at dusk, you might glimpse a shy, rabbit-sized mammal. The Jamaican coney, or hutia, is one of many animal species that are unique to the island. Just how the hutia came to live on Jamaica is an amazing story, for its ancestors must have arrived either by swimming or by drifting on

GOING BATTY

Bats first flew to Jamaica millions of years ago. They may have been blown across the sea by storm winds. There are now 25 species living on the island, each one with its own diet. Some are insect eaters, while others feed on fruit or nectar, spreading seeds and pollen that help plants to reproduce. In Jamaica, bats are commonly called "rat-bats." Some roost in treeholes, others in attics or church steeples. Many dwell in caves. The dark caves of Cockpit Country host huge populations of bats, with up to 50,000 in a single cave. At dusk the bats stream out in dark clouds to hunt moths, which confusingly are also called rat-bats! The floors of these

▲ Bats fly out of their caves at dusk.

caves are covered in a deep layer of guano, or bat droppings. Islanders collect this smelly substance to fertilize crops.

DRAGONS AND CROCODILES

In 1990 a hiker walking in the dry Hellshire Hills near Kingston came face-to-face with a 5-foot (1.5-m) lizard! This discovery caused a sensation, not only because the hiker claimed to have found a "dragon," but also because the giant ground iguana of Jamaica was thought to have died out 50 years earlier. The immense reptile (below) is one of several on the island. Equally spectacular is the Jamaican alligator, which is a subspecies of the American crocodile. These crocs grow to 13 feet (4 m) long. Jamaica also has darting geckoes and anole lizards, which signal to one another by flicking their throat flaps. There are several nonpoisonous snakes, including the large yellow boa.

◄ A Jamaican iguana, one of the largest lizards in the world

floating vegetation. The hutia is now rare because it is hunted by a predator that is fairly new to Jamaica—the mongoose. This hunter was brought to the island in the 1870s to kill rats. However, the mongoose also turned to hunting hutias and stealing the eggs of birds and reptiles.

Big Butterflies

The highlands of Jamaica are home to the homerus swallowtail —the largest butterfly in the Americas. With a wingspan measuring 6 inches (25 cm) across, this insect is bigger than several of the island's birds. The swallowtail is an example of a form of evolution quite common on islands called gigantism. Like the Jamaican iguana, the butterflies have evolved to a large size, probably to take advantage of food sources. With their black and yellow markings, these butterflies are very rare, partly because so many have been caught by specimen hunters. They are now protected by law.

Coastal Kingdoms

Jamaica's coastal habitats include mangrove forests, whose trees live halfway between land and water. The tangled roots of mangrove trees stick out of the mud, sheltering fish and shellfish, such as crabs. The swamps of the southern coasts are home to crocodiles and West Indian manatees. These large, gentle mammals, also known as sea cows, are very scarce because they were widely hunted for meat.

▲ The roots of mangrove trees poke out of the Black River.

Hawksbill and loggerhead turtles nest on remote beaches and offshore islands called cays. The coral reefs that fringe the shores are home to a variety of marine life. Large predatory fish such as tuna, marlin, nurse sharks, and the dreaded barracuda patrol the deep waters on the ocean side of the reefs.

▼ The Jamaican tody is known by local people as a robin because of its bright red throat.

Bird Paradise

Jamaica is also rich in birdlife. It is home to nearly 30 endemic kinds of birds, some of which only live in particular parts of the island. Visitors come from around the world to try to catch sight of endemic species such as the orangequit and Jamaican oreole.

The *Fight* for *Freedom*

N THE PORT OF MONTEGO BAY stands a reminder of Jamaica's past: Sam Sharpe Square. For 300 years, the island's wealth came from slave labor. Under Spanish and then English rule, African slaves were harshly treated. At Christmas 1831 a slave from Montego Bay named Sam Sharpe led an uprising. Across Jamaica 200,000 slaves rebelled, burning estates and planters' houses. The English army put down the Christmas Rebellion with great force. Sharpe and 500 of his supporters were hanged in Montego Bay's city square. However, in Britain people were sickened by the brutality, and before the decade was out slavery was abolished. Today Sam Sharpe is a national hero. His statue stands in the square where he died, renamed in his honor.

◀ **This statue of Sam Sharpe stands in Sam Sharpe Square, Montego Bay. The small building in back was once the Cage, a jail used to imprison escaped slaves.**

CENTURIES OF STRUGGLE

People called the Taino arrived in Jamaica from South America in the seventh century A.D. In 1494 Christopher Columbus landed on the island during his second expedition to the "New World." The first European settlers were Spaniards arriving from Hispaniola in 1510. They set up plantations and built their first capital, Sevilla Nueva (New Seville), on the north coast. However, in 1534 the Spanish moved the capital to a southern site, now known as Spanish Town.

In 1670 Jamaica was taken over by the English. The island became a center of sugar production, run by

slaves. British plantation owners were known for their cruelty. One writer, Charles Leslie, noted in *A New and Exact Account of Jamaica* (1740), "No Country exceeds them in barbarous treatment of slaves, or in the cruel Methods that they put them to death." Over the next 150 years there were many slave rebellions before slavery was finally abolished in Jamaica in 1838.

▶ **Most Africans brought to work as slaves on Jamaican plantations could only expect to live for about seven years.**

Time line

This chart shows the approximate dates of events in Jamaica since A.D. 1300

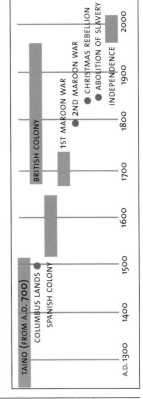

TAINO (FROM A.D. 700)
COLUMBUS LANDS
SPANISH COLONY
BRITISH COLONY
1ST MAROON WAR
2ND MAROON WAR
CHRISTMAS REBELLION
ABOLITION OF SLAVERY
INDEPENDENCE

A.D. 1300 1400 1500 1600 1700 1800 1900 2000

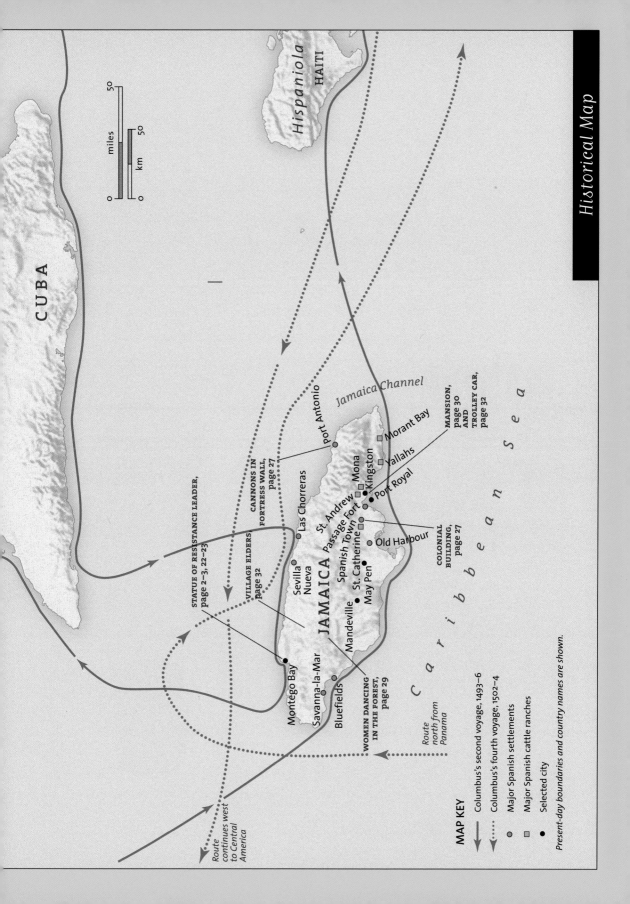

Historical Map

CUBA

Hispaniola

HAITI

Jamaica Channel

STATUE OF RESISTANCE LEADER,
page 2–3, 22–23

CANNONS IN
FORTRESS WALL,
page 27

VILLAGE ELDERS
page 32

Port Antonio

Las Chorreras

Morant Bay

MANSION,
page 30
AND
TROLLEY CAR,
page 32

Sevilla
Nueva

St. Andrew   Mona
Passage Fort Kingston   Yallahs
Spanish Town   Port Royal
St. Catherine
Old Harbour

JAMAICA

Mandeville   May Pen

COLONIAL
BUILDING,
page 27

Montego Bay

Savanna-la-Mar

Bluefields

WOMEN DANCING
IN THE FOREST,
page 29

C a r i b b e a n   S e a

Route
north from
Panama

Route
continues west
to Central
America

miles   50
0

0   km   50

MAP KEY

Columbus's second voyage, 1493–6

Columbus's fourth voyage, 1502–4

Major Spanish settlements

Major Spanish cattle ranches

Selected city

Present-day boundaries and country names are shown.

A Spanish Colony

As far as we know, nobody lived on Jamaica until the mid-seventh century, when people called the Taino arrived. Some experts think the Taino were Arawaks, members of an ethnic group from South America.

The first European settlers were Spaniards who arrived about 850 years later. Like other pioneers of that time, many of the immigrants were looking for treasure and hoping to get rich quick. The Spanish found no riches, but Jamaica became a valuable supply base for ships making the journey between Europe and Spain's empire in South America.

THE TAINO

The Taino came originally from the Orinoco River region in Venezuela. They reached Jamaica in dug-out canoes, arriving in two separate waves of migration, around A.D. 650 and 870. The Taino settled in the fertile valleys by the sea and lived by fishing, gathering food, and farming crops such as cassava, cotton, and tobacco. Most of what we know of the Taino comes from their stone sculptures and cave paintings, which have survived until modern times. Historians estimate that in 1490 there were as many as 500,000 Taino on Jamaica. Huge numbers died of harsh treatment and European diseases over the next few decades. They were virtually wiped out by 1600.

▶ A Taino wood carving of a bird used in religious ceremonies in the 15th century

The Spanish community also began to farm bananas and sugarcane. They enslaved the Taino, who began to die in large numbers from overwork and diseases introduced from Europe. The Spaniards imported hired workers from home and also forced Africans to work as slaves.

▲ A government building in Spanish Town has the old-fashioned architecture used in Spanish colonies.

England Takes Over

The British were jealous of Spain's wealthy colonies in the Caribbean. In 1654 the British leader Oliver Cromwell sent a fleet of ships to capture territory in the region. In 1655, the British seized Jamaica. Spanish attempts to retake the island failed, and in 1670 the territory was officially handed to England as part of a peace deal with Spain.

However, a few pockets of resistance remained. Groups of former slaves, who became known as Maroons, had set up bases in the mountains. For the next 150 years these rebels held out against the English, defying repeated attempts to defeat them.

▼ A cannon pokes through the wall at Fort George in Port Antonio, a harbor founded by the British.

BUCCANEERS' BASE

In the 1660s Port Royal became a base for British pirates who terrorized the Caribbean Sea. Soon the British governor of Jamaica, Thomas Modyford, licensed the pirates, or "privateers," to harass the ports and ships of rival countries. Thanks to the pirates, Port Royal became very wealthy. It was known as "the wickedest city in the world." In 1671 a Welsh pirate named Henry Morgan sacked the Spanish colony of Panama—but England was then at peace with Spain. Modyford was fired—but the British decided to make the most of Morgan's leadership skills. He was knighted and made Jamaica's new governor. Piracy in Jamaica continued for another 50 years. Famous pirates included Blackbeard, who fought with lit fuses in his beard, and Calico Jack, who was helped by the female pirates Mary Read and Anne Bonney. In 1720 Calico Jack was captured and executed in Jamaica. His body was placed in a cage, or gibbet, and hung at the entrance to Port Royal harbor as a warning that piracy was no longer tolerated on the island.

▲ Blackbeard and his crew fight the British Navy in the pirate's last—and fatal—battle in 1718.

The early part of British rule over Jamaica was a period of lawlessness. Pirates controlled Jamaica's biggest port, Port Royal, and pillaged and plundered across the Caribbean. During the 18th century, the island settled down and grew into one of the most prosperous colonies in the region. The source of the wealth was sugarcane. Coffee-drinking was in fashion in Europe, which made sugar such a valuable crop that it was called "white gold."

Thousands of new settlers arrived from Britain, lured by the chance of making a fortune, and between 1673 and 1740 the number of plantations increased from 57 to 430. A huge workforce was needed to run the plantations, and so, like the Spanish, the British imported Africans to work as slaves.

The Slave Trade

By the late 1700s Jamaica had become one of the largest slave markets in the Western Hemisphere. Slave ships made a three-step voyage between Europe, West Africa, and Jamaica or other places in the Americas. This was known as the Triangular Trade. On the "Middle Passage"—the part of the voyage

▲ A receipt for slaves sold to a planter in Jamaica

THE MAROONS

When Spanish settlers left Jamaica in 1655 to escape the English, they let their slaves go. The freed workers escaped to the remote mountains. They became known as Maroons from the Spanish word *cimarrones*, which means "untamed." The runaways fled to the Blue Mountains in the east. They were led by a queen named Nanny. In 1690, more runaways established a second base in Cockpit Country. The two groups united and won independence from the British authorities in 1739. However, the Maroons were beaten in a second war with the British in 1795. After their defeat,

▲ People from a Maroon village celebrate Cudjoe Day, a festival remembering a Maroon leader.

most Maroons went back to their villages, but 600 were deported, first to Nova Scotia in Canada and then to Sierra Leone in West Africa. These were the first slaves to be sent back to Africa from the New World.

▼ Devon House near Kingston was the home of George Stiebel, the son of a German and Jamaican who became the island's first black millionaire in the 1870s. The house is built in the grand style used by plantation owners.

between Africa and America—newly captured slaves were chained below deck in cramped conditions without sanitation or enough food. About one in five slaves died during the two-month crossing. Those that survived were sold at market to the highest bidder. Most Jamaican planters forced their slaves to work very hard. The slaves usually died after only a few years in the plantations. The landowners could replace slaves easily and did not need to ensure they were healthy. Between 1700 and 1807, 600,000 African slaves were brought to Jamaica.

Slave Rebellions

As a reaction to their harsh treatment, slaves often started rebellions. In 1690 a group of runaway slaves joined the Maroons in the highlands, and began an attack on the English known as the First Maroon War. The Maroons made guerrilla-style attacks on the English for nearly 40 years, before the British made peace with the rebels. The peace treaty gave the Maroons 1,500 acres (610 hectares) of wild country for their own. In return they agreed to help the British recapture runaway slaves and to put down any future rebellions. When a former African chief named Tacky led a major slave uprising in 1760, the Maroons fought against the rebels.

The truce between the Maroons and the British lasted about 50 years, but in 1795 a second war was sparked by the public flogging of two Maroons. This time the English brought in bloodhounds to pursue the rebel fighters through the hills. Eventually the Maroons were forced to surrender.

The End of Slavery

During the late 1700s the antislavery movement gathered strength in Britain and the Americas. In 1807 it became illegal to capture new slaves and sell them anywhere in the British Empire. However, slaves already working in British colonies were not freed. In 1831, the violent defeat of the Christmas Rebellion led by Sam Sharpe gave a final boost to the antislavery movement. In 1838 all Jamaican slaves were freed. The British government paid £20 million (worth about

▼ Sugar cutters take a rest from their work in 1910. Although slavery had ended more than 70 years before, many African Jamaicans still worked on the plantations.

$370 million dollars today) to plantation owners to pay for the loss of their workers.

Troubled Times

Over the next several decades life remained hard for the freed slaves. Some were able to rent plots of land and set up "free villages," but many had to work in the plantations for low pay. In 1846 the sugar industry was damaged when Britain raised taxes on Jamaican sugar being imported to Britain. Jamaican sugar had previously benefited from low taxes; now it cost the same as sugar imported from other countries.

In 1865 tensions between African Jamaicans and those of European descent erupted in a revolt called the Morant Bay Rebellion. Rebels led by Paul Bogle marched on the courthouse in Morant Bay. When the police opened fire, a riot broke out. Bogle and 430 rebels were executed, and thousands of people were flogged. The British government was shocked by the violence. It had largely left Jamaica to run itself, but now it decided to rule the island from London.

Independence at Last

In the early 20th century Jamaicans had begun to press for independence from Britain. In 1938, after many riots and protests, a labor leader named

▲ A 1925 postcard shows a streetcar in Kingston.

▼ Until the 1960s Maroon villages were ruled by chiefs, such as Colonel Robertson, the leader of Cockpit Country Maroons.

VOYAGE ON THE *WINDRUSH*

In the 1950s a quarter million Jamaicans left their homes and traveled to Britain to find work. A boat called the *Empire Windrush* has a special place in Jamaican and British history as the ship that carried the first group of these emigrants to Britain in 1948. *Windrush* passenger Oswald "Columbus" Denniston reported: "Word went round that this boat was taking passengers for a cheap fare to go to Britain. It was common knowledge that there was work in Britain just after the war." Another *Windrush* passenger, Vince Reid, said: "My parents brought me on the *Windrush*—they came in search of a better life. I was 13 when I arrived. It was quite an experience. At school I came across real hostility. I am 62 years old now. I have been in Britain for 50 years. I prefer to live here. Well, my family is here, my wife, my grandchildren are here." Today 1 percent of Britons are of Caribbean descent.

▲ The *Empire Windrush* arrives in London with 482 Jamaicans on board.

Alexander Bustamente founded the first trade union in the Caribbean. Bustamente's cousin, Norman Manley, founded a political party called the People's National Party (PNP), which was linked to the union. In 1943 Bustamente broke away from the PNP and formed a new party, the Jamaican Labour Party (JLP). These two parties have dominated Jamaican politics ever since.

During World War II (1939–1945) Jamaicans fought on the side of Britain and its ally the United States. Jamaican leaders continued to ask for independence. In 1944 Jamaica formed its own parliament. The JLP won the first election. In 1959 Jamaica became self-governing, with Norman Manley as prime minister. In 1962 Jamaica finally gained full independence, and Alexander Bustamente became prime minister.

Ragged Music

R EGGAE, OR "RAGGED MUSIC," is perhaps Jamaica's best-known export. Today it is a truly international musical style. Its rhythms and bass lines influence musicians across the world. The sound emerged in Jamaica in the 1950s, born of the musical styles mento, ska, and rocksteady. The name came later, from a 1968 song by Toots and the Maytals named "Do the Reggay."

The roll call of Jamaica's reggae stars includes Desmond Dekker, Jimmy Cliff, Peter Tosh, and Burning Spear. The most famous star of all was Bob Marley, backed by his group the Wailers. Marley sang about the hardships and injustices of ghetto life. Marley is loved across Jamaica, but today you are more likely to hear dancehall music, the latest offshoot of reggae.

◀ Bob Marley was Jamaica's most successful musician. His album *Legend* sold 12 million copies worldwide, more than any other reggae album.

JAMAICA'S PEOPLE

Jamaica has about 2.7 million people. Just over half live in cities. Country dwellers used to outnumber city folk, but recently people have been moving in from rural areas to find work in towns. Kingston, Jamaica's capital and largest city, holds about a third of the population. In addition, there are about 2 million Jamaicans and their descendants living abroad, mainly in the United States, Canada, and Britain.

About 91 percent of Jamaicans are of African descent, while 7 percent are of mixed African and European descent. Over the centuries, many other people have come to Jamaica to find work, including Chinese, Indians, Syrians, and Germans. Jamaica is proud of its varied heritage—the country's motto is "Out of Many, One People."

▼ Montego Bay is Jamaica's second-largest city, followed by Spanish Town.

Common Jamaican Phrases

Jamaica's official language is English, but most people speak "patois" or "creole." This is a blend of the English dialect that was spoken by the planters and words from West Africa and several other languages thrown in. Here are a few phrases that will help you get by in Jamaica.

Hello	Yao [also Yush]
I'm feeling good	Irie
Don't worry about it	Feel no way
Everything's fine	Cool runnings
See you later	Likkle more
Safe journey	Walk good

1950 / 1.4 million — 24% urban / 76% rural

1970 / 1.9 million — 42% urban / 58% rural

1990 / 2.4 million — 51% urban / 49% rural

2005 / 2.7 million — 52% urban / 48% rural

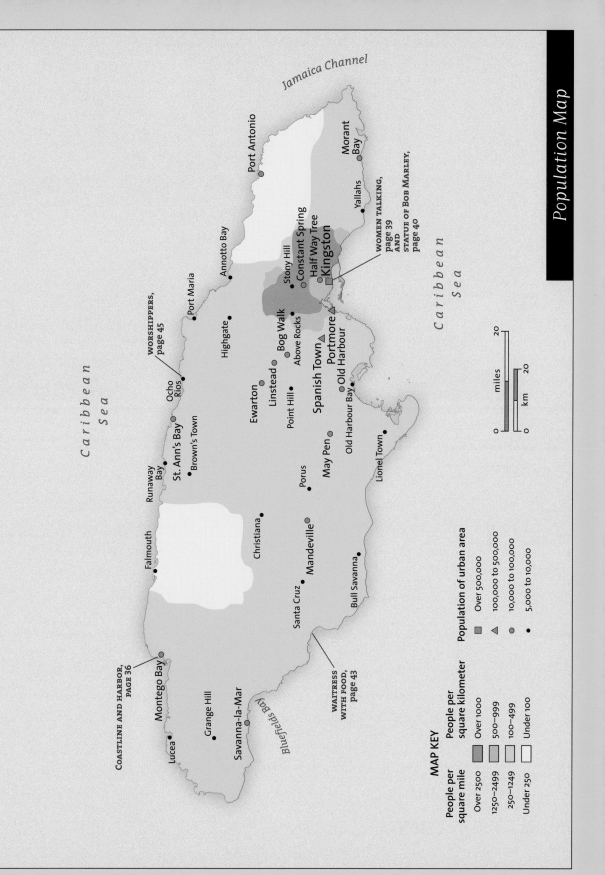

Population Map

Jamaica Channel

Caribbean
Sea

Caribbean
Sea

Port Antonio

Morant
Bay

Yallahs

Annotto Bay

Constant Spring
Stony Hill
Half Way Tree
Kingston

WOMEN TALKING,
page 39
AND
STATUE OF BOB MARLEY,
page 40

Port Maria

Highgate

Bog Walk
Above Rocks
Spanish Town
Portmore
Old Harbour

Linstead

Ewarton

Point Hill

Old Harbour Bay

WORSHIPPERS,
page 45

Ocho
Rios

Brown's Town

St. Ann's Bay

Runaway
Bay

Porus

May Pen

Lionel Town

Falmouth

Christiana

Mandeville

Santa Cruz

Bull Savanna

WAITRESS
WITH FOOD,
page 43

Montego Bay

COASTLINE AND HARBOR,
PAGE 36

Lucea

Grange Hill

Savanna-la-Mar

Bluefields Bay

0   miles   20

0   km   20

MAP KEY

People per square mile	People per square kilometer
Over 2500	Over 1000
1250–2499	500–999
250–1249	100–499
Under 250	Under 100

Population of urban area

Over 500,000

100,000 to 500,000

10,000 to 100,000

5,000 to 10,000

▲ Students line up
outside their country
schoolhouse.

Extending the Family

Jamaican families are sometimes organized in a
different way from those in many other parts of the
world. In addition to families with two parents and
their children, there are also large extended families
in which grandparents or other relatives help to look
after several children. Single-parent families are also
common, usually made up of a mother raising
children. It is not uncommon for Jamaican women to
bring up children on their own, or with the help of
their family, before marrying. Some parents leave their
children in the care of a relative or guardian while they
go to work abroad.

All children receive six years of free schooling
between the ages of 5 and 11. Before that, most

JONKONNU

At Christmas Jamaicans of all ages take to the streets for the masked parade of Jonkonnu. Figures with giant heads lead the parade. They represent spirits and mythical characters such as Horsehead, Belly-Woman, and Pitchy Patchy. The figures are followed by throngs of "set girls" in colored sashes, all dancing to flute and drum music. They cry "Jonkonnu a come!" as they have done since colonial times. Also spelled John Canoe, the parade may be named after a black merchant from the colonial period, but no one is quite sure. The roots of the event lie in African rituals, which use singing and dancing to communicate with spirits, who are sometimes represented by masks.

▲ Dancers in colorful costumes celebrate Jonkonnu.

attend nursery school. At 10 or 11, pupils take an exam. The results are used to decide which type of secondary school they will go on to. About two-thirds of the pupils spend another five years in high school. The school day lasts from 8 a.m. to at least 3 p.m., with about 30 students to a class. Students may then go on to study at one of Jamaica's universities or colleges. These schools charge fees, but there are scholarships available.

▼ Edna Manley (far right) listens to Louise Bennett (left), a famous Jamaican storyteller, in 1963.

Island Art

Jamaica has had a strong tradition of sculpture since the Taino. The most famous sculptor of

recent times was Edna Manley, who was the wife of Jamaica's first prime minister, Norman Manley. Painter Colin Garland and potter Cecil Baugh are also well known. One of the best places to see Jamaican art is at the National Gallery in Kingston. The Jamaican Festival held every summer is a great opportunity to get acquainted with Jamaican arts, music, and dance.

Many styles of dancing in Jamaica, such as myal, revival, and quadrille, blend African and European influences. Jamaican modern dance is influenced by all of these and also by classical ballet and European modern dance. The country's best-known dance troupe is the National Dance Theatre Company.

Jamaican Sounds

Music is the lifeblood of Jamaica. You hear its pulse around almost every corner. African drum rhythms have had a big influence on reggae, dancehall, ska, mento, dub, and other Jamaican styles that are popular all over the world.

Reggae is the best-known style of all. It developed in the 1960s in working-class parts of Jamaica. In the early 1970s it reached an international audience for the first time through the movie *The Harder They Come*, which starred Jamaican musician Jimmy Cliff. The biggest reggae star, Bob Marley, had

▲ A statue of Bob Marley stands in Kingston.

many international hits. He died from cancer in 1981, but his music remains very popular. Jamaica's biggest reggae festival is Reggae Sumfest, held in Montego Bay in July. Reggae, and more recently dancehall, is also played at mobile

discos, often outdoors, called "sound stages." In the late 1970s sound stages were imported to the United States. They became an important part of the emergence of hip-hop culture.

Taking It Easy

Jamaica has a sociable culture. In their free time Jamaicans often get together to enjoy themselves. The warm, sunny climate means that a lot of life goes on outdoors. With Jamaica's beautiful beaches, it is no surprise that fishing is a popular pastime.

Many people just hang out on the porch with friends and family, catching up on the latest gossip. The more

▲ Jamaica's national soccer team—nicknamed the "Reggae Boyz"— prepare to play Croatia in the World Cup in 1998.

▼ The fastest man on earth, Jamaican Asafa Powell, celebrates his world-record 100-meter sprint in 2007.

COOL RUNNINGS

In 1988 Jamaica entered a four-man bobsled team in the Winter Olympics held in Calgary, Canada. The entry was unexpected from a warm, tropical island with no history of winter sports! The team that arrived in Calgary had practiced in carts in the Jamaican hills, but most of them had never seen snow. They finished in 29th position but won the respect of the crowd. In 1993 the story was made into a movie called *Cool Runnings*. The title comes from the patois greeting that means—what else?—"stay cool." In 1994 the Jamaican bobsled team came in 14th in the Winter Olympics in Lillehammer, Norway. Fans are hoping that the best is still to come.

▲ The Jamaican bobsled team competes in Norway.

energetic play soccer, cricket, or basketball on any patch of open ground. Older people and some youngsters enjoy dominoes or draughts (checkers).

Speed and Skill

Jamaicans are passionate about sports. Soccer, cricket, basketball, and netball, a game a little like basketball, are all favorites. In 1998 there were great celebrations when the national soccer team, the Reggae Boyz, reached the finals of the World Cup for the first time.

Jamaicans also represent their country at cricket but as members of the West Indies team, which includes players from across the Caribbean. There is high excitement among cricket fans when arch rival England comes to play the West Indies in a "test match" at Jamaica's main cricket pitch, Sabina Park in Kingston. The West Indies dominated world cricket in the 1980s, and the sport used to be Jamaica's favorite. Today, however, many boys and girls prefer to play basketball or soccer, and Jamaica is no longer a leading cricket nation. The Jamaican women's netball team ranks among the best in the world.

Jamaica has produced a long line of sprint champions, including Asafa Powell, who broke the men's 100-meter record in 2007. Jamaica has one of the highest proportions of Olympic-medal winners for its population in the world. Most Jamaican success in sports comes from athletics.

Eating in Jamaica

Jamaican cooking is a delicious blend of African, Chinese, Indian, and European styles. Jamaicans like their food spicy, with plenty of garlic, chili pepper, and allspice, which comes from pimento. The national dish, saltfish and ackee, is made with salted cod and ackee—a fruit that looks and tastes a lot like scrambled eggs when it is cooked. Saltfish and ackee is

NATIONAL HOLIDAYS

Jamaica's public holidays include Christian festivals and days commemorating landmarks in history, such as Independence Day. Even festivals such as Christmas are a little different in Jamaica, with carols sung to a reggae beat!

NEW YEAR'S DAY:	January 1
EASTER:	March / April
LABOUR DAY:	May 23
EMANCIPATION DAY:	August 1 (the day when slaves gained their freedom)
INDEPENDENCE DAY:	August 6
NATIONAL HEROES' DAY:	Third Monday in October (part of a week-long festival celebrating Jamaican culture)
CHRISTMAS DAY:	December 25
BOXING DAY:	December 26

▼ A waitress offers a plate of ackee and saltfish, a Jamaican dish.

RASTAFARIANISM

▲ A Rastafarian family

Rastafarianism is a faith that grew up in Jamaica in the 1930s to counter the unequal treatment of blacks. The religion's prophet, civil-rights activist Marcus Garvey, foretold the crowning of an African king who would be the savior of all African peoples and lead them home. Rastafarians believe that this savior was Haile Selassie, emperor of Ethiopia from 1916 to 1974. They believe he was a direct descendant of King Solomon, who is mentioned in the Bible.

Most Rastafarians regard Africa as a spiritual rather than a physical home. They compare the Caribbean with Babylon, the land where the Jews were forced into exile in the Bible. Rasta men wear their hair in "dreadlocks," following an Old Testament verse that warns that hair should not be cut. Clothes, especially hats, sport the red, gold, and green colors of the Ethiopian flag.

▼ People arrive at a tin-roofed church in rural Jamaica for a service.

eaten for breakfast and also on Sundays, along with yams, dumplings, and plantains (similar to bananas). Most other meals are eaten with rice and peas seasoned with onions and coconut milk.

Jamaica is famous for a dish called jerk meat. This is pork, chicken, or fish soaked in herbs and spices and then cooked over a fire of pimento wood until it is bursting with flavor. Chinese and Indian dishes, such as curried goat, are also popular. Other Jamaican recipes have mysterious names: rundown is fish cooked in coconut while stamp-n-go is a fried fish pancake. To finish up there is always a wide range of juicy and colorful tropical fruits.

A Spiritual Side

Most people in Jamaica follow some form of religion. About 62 percent are Christians. Of these, most are Protestants, including Baptists, Seventh-Day Adventists, Pentecostalists, Anglicans, and a group called the Church of God. About 100,000 Jamaicans are Rastafarians, a faith closely linked to Christianity.

Jamaica is believed to have more churches per square mile than any other country. Most people attend church on Sunday and many children go to Sunday school. Jamaican services are lively, with singing and clapping.

About 35 percent of the population follow non-Christian faiths, which include Hinduism, Judaism, and Islam. This group also includes many Jamaicans who follow home-grown faiths that have African roots, such as Kumina and Pocomania.

SMALL MADNESS

Pocomania was the semisecret religion of Jamaica's African slaves. After slavery was abolished, Pocomania was practiced more openly. Like many other aspects of Jamaican culture, it blends African and European traditions. Followers believe in the existence of spirits who have the power to influence our world. The Christian Holy Spirit is a powerful member of these spirits. In the chief ritual, followers use drumming, chanting, and dancing to enter a trance and communicate with the spirits. The name Pocomania means "small madness."

▲ Followers of Pocomania at worship

A City
by
the Sea

KINGSTON IS ONE OF THE LARGEST, most lively cities in the Caribbean. The capital of Jamaican culture as well as the center of its government, it pulses to reggae music night and day. With a fine natural harbor and backed by the Blue Mountains, modern Kingston sprawls over the coastal plain. It is really several cities in one. The downtown area by the shore is the oldest district, with wharves and markets lining the waterfront. Colonial buildings here include several theaters and concert halls. To the north, leafy New Kingston is the business district. The city is ringed by crowded slum areas, such as Trench Town and Jones Town, where crime is never far away. Jamaica as a whole has the same contrasts—great natural beauty but also widespread poverty.

◀ **Kingston is home to a third of Jamaica's entire population, but compared to other capitals, the city has only a few large buildings.**

LOCAL GOVERNMENT

Under British rule, Jamaica was divided into three counties with very English-sounding names: Cornwall, Middlesex, and Surrey. Today these old boundaries are less important. For administrative purposes Jamaica is divided into 14 parishes, as shown on the map. Each is run by a local council, which is responsible for services such as health, education, transportation, and the upkeep of parks. Parish councillors are elected for three years. The parishes of Kingston and St. Andrew together form the Kingston Metropolitan Area.

Jamaica's currency is the Jamaican dollar, which is divided into 100 cents.

Jamaica is a member of the Caribbean Community and Common Market (CARICOM for short), which makes trade between Caribbean nations easier. The country also has long-standing trade links with the United Kingdom.

Trading Partners

Jamaica's main trading links are with North America, Europe, and other Caribbean countries. The United States is both the main source of goods coming into the country, and also its main export market. Jamaica's primary exports include sugar, bananas, coffee, citrus fruits, yams, rum, and aluminum ore. The country's chief imports include machinery, transportation equipment, construction materials, oil and other fuels, food, chemicals, and fertilizers.

Country	Percent Jamaica exports
United States	30.2%
Canada	15.6%
China	15.2%
All others combined	39.0%

Country	Percent Jamaica imports
United States	39.3%
Trinidad and Tobago	13.6%
Venezuela	9.5%
All others combined	37.6%

▼ Jamaicans buy fresh fruit grown on the island from a market stall in Montego Bay.

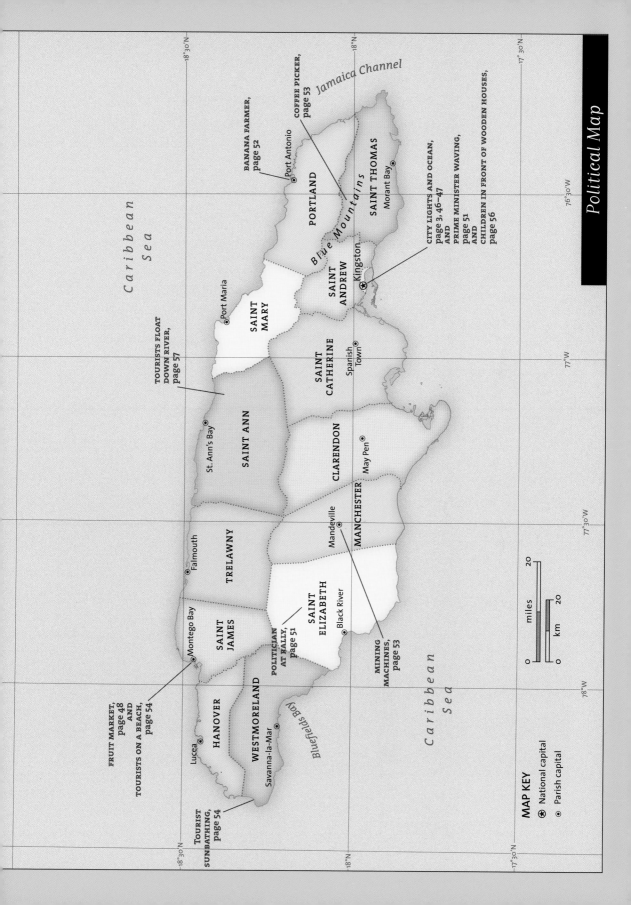

Political Map

MAP KEY

⊛ National capital
⊙ Parish capital

Caribbean Sea

Caribbean Sea

Jamaica Channel

Bluefields Bay

Blue Mountains

miles 0 20
km 0 20

HANOVER
Lucea ⊙

WESTMORELAND
Savanna-la-Mar ⊙

SAINT JAMES
Montego Bay ⊙

TRELAWNY
Falmouth ⊙

SAINT ELIZABETH
Black River ⊙

SAINT ANN
St. Ann's Bay ⊙

MANCHESTER
Mandeville ⊙

CLARENDON
May Pen ⊙

SAINT CATHERINE
Spanish Town ⊙

SAINT MARY
Port Maria ⊙

PORTLAND
Port Antonio ⊙

SAINT ANDREW
Kingston ⊛

SAINT THOMAS
Morant Bay ⊙

TOURIST SUNBATHING, page 54

FRUIT MARKET, page 48 AND TOURISTS ON A BEACH, page 54

POLITICIAN AT RALLY, page 51

MINING MACHINES, page 53

TOURISTS FLOAT DOWN RIVER, page 57

BANANA FARMER, page 52

COFFEE PICKER, page 53

CITY LIGHTS AND OCEAN, page 3, 46–47, AND PRIME MINISTER WAVING, page 51 AND CHILDREN IN FRONT OF WOODEN HOUSES, page 56

Going It Alone

Jamaica is one of the oldest democracies in the Caribbean. Violence has sometimes flared at election times, but calm usually returns when results are announced. Since independence in 1962 two parties have dominated Jamaican politics. The People's National Party (PNP) describes itself as a democratic socialist party. The Jamaican Labour Party (JLP) is a pro-business party.

In 1972 the PNP, which was then led by Michael Manley, son of its founder Norman Manley, took power. Michael Manley had a background in labor

HOW THE GOVERNMENT WORKS

Because Jamaica is a member of the British Commonwealth, its official head of state is currently the British queen. She is represented in Jamaica by a governor general, but his role is mainly ceremonial. Jamaica is a parliamentary democracy. The prime minister, who leads the party with the most seats in parliament, heads the government. He or she appoints a cabinet of ministers to run different departments, such as health and foreign affairs. The parliament is made up of two houses, the Senate and House of Representatives. The Senate has 21 members, 13 of whom are chosen by the prime minister, 8 by the main opposition party. The House of Representatives has 60 members elected by public vote every five years. The highest court is the Supreme Court. Judges are appointed by the parliament.

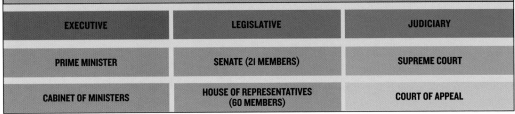

GOVERNOR GENERAL		
EXECUTIVE	LEGISLATIVE	JUDICIARY
PRIME MINISTER	SENATE (21 MEMBERS)	SUPREME COURT
CABINET OF MINISTERS	HOUSE OF REPRESENTATIVES (60 MEMBERS)	COURT OF APPEAL

politics, and was committed to improving conditions for all Jamaicans. His government increased spending on health and education. However, Manley also tried to distance Jamaica from the United States, and this discouraged foreign companies from investing in the island. By the late 1970s the country had severe economic problems.

Changing Leaders

In 1980 the JLP, led by Edward Seaga, was swept into power. Seaga immediately restored friendly relations with the United States and began to rebuild the economy. Business started to pick up.

In 1989 Michael Manley returned to power, but his political ideas were now very different. His government continued the pro-business policies of the JLP and good relations with the United States. The PNP held on to power right through the 1990s and into the 21st century. When Manley retired in 1992, Jamaica elected its first black prime minister, P. J. Patterson. In 2006 Portia Simpson Miller took over the leadership of the PNP, becoming

▲ P. J. Patterson, Jamaica's first black prime minister, talks to his supporters.

▼ Portia Simpson Miller, the island's first female leader, ran Jamaica between 2006 and 2007.

Jamaica's first woman prime minister. However, in 2007 the PNP's long 18-year reign was ended by the JLP under a new leader, Bruce Golding.

Old Trades, New Businesses

Jamaica's economy is still recovering from problems that followed independence. Agriculture is one of the main industries, but mining and tourism have now been added to the list.

▲ Freshly cut bananas are loaded onto a truck for transport to market. Most Jamaican bananas are exported.

About a fifth of Jamaica's workers are involved in farming, forestry, or fishing. The most important crop is still sugarcane, but Jamaica also produces bananas, citrus fruits, ackee, coconut, pimento, coffee, cacao, and yams. Jamaican farms rear chickens and goats for meat, and cattle for both meat and milk. The main breed of cattle, called Jamaica Hope, yields more milk than other breeds found in similarly warm places. Jamaica also exports fish and shellfish. However, the country is not able to grow all of its own food and so has to import some from abroad.

Digging It

Mining is very important to Jamaica's economy. The country is a leading producer of the mineral bauxite, which is used to make aluminum. The sale of bauxite

BANKING ON BAUXITE

Bauxite is a red mineral that contains about 50 percent aluminum oxide. Jamaica's deposits of bauxite were first mined in the 1950s. The valuable mineral is mainly mined at the surface in open pits. The pits leave lakes of red mud, which scar the landscape in places. The ore is transported to factories where it is washed, crushed, and dried to form a powder. The powder is moved to another plant to be refined into alumina (pure aluminum oxide). Alumina is smelted to produce aluminum. However, the last process requires so much energy it is not economic to do it in Jamaica, so it is shipped to plants abroad. Jamaica's bauxite mines are all owned by North American companies. Together they produce over 11 million tons (10 million tonnes) of bauxite a year.

▲ An immense power shovel digs up bauxite.

provides about half of all Jamaica's export earnings. Gypsum is also mined in Jamaica. The country has few energy sources and so it relies on buying fuel from other countries. Jamaican factories produce cement, chemicals, clothes, and machinery.

▼ A woman picks coffee cherries on a plantation in the hills. The cherries contain the beans used to make coffee.

Dream Destination

Tourism is one of Jamaica's key sources of income. Every year about one million tourists visit the island. Most of the visitors are wealthy people from Europe and North America. Tourism is well developed. Many people associate Jamaica with lazy beach vacations, but there is a huge amount for visitors to do. At leading resorts such as

Montego Bay, Negril, and Ocho Rios, they can skim over the sea in a sailboat or sailboard. People can explore the beautiful coral reefs by snorkeling or scuba diving, or head out to sea to try their luck at sport fishing.

Jamaica's tourist attractions are not all on the coast. Inland visitors go rafting on the rivers and take a dip at a waterfall or other scenic area. Taking horseback rides into the Blue Mountains is another popular activity. Resorts have golf courses, tennis courts, and many other sporting facilities. Some tourists like to explore Jamaica's historic towns, pirate haunts, and plantations. The tourist industry is a major employer, with thousands of Jamaicans working in hotels or as guides.

▲ A tourist relaxes at a luxury resort on the Jamaican coast.

▼ Vacationers enjoy themselves on one of Jamaica's many beaches.

SUGAR, SUGAR

Sugar has been Jamaica's chief crop since the 1600s. Sugarcane is a type of tall grass. Beneath the tough rind, the long stalks contain sugary fibers. In Jamaica the cane is harvested between November and June. It is transported by road or rail to mills, where it is crushed between rollers to produce sweet, cloudy, cane juice. This juice is then heated and processed to make sugar crystals. A by-product of this process is thick, syrupy molasses, which is used to make Jamaica's famous rum. The Jamaican sugar industry has been in trouble since the 1960s. Efforts are being made to solve this: A fuel called ethanol can also be made from sugarcane. This clean-burning fuel could help to solve Jamaica's needs for energy and reduce the vast sums of money it spends on importing oil.

▲ Cut sugarcane is washed before being processed into sugar at a plant in Jamaica.

Getting Around

Most people use buses to move around Jamaica. The country has good roads but not many cars outside of the cities. In Kingston, however, traffic congestion has recently become a major problem. Buses are frequent but can get very crowded at busy times. People also use minibuses and taxis. Whatever the vehicle, driving is often slow-going. Country and even city roads are sometimes blocked by herds of goats or a line of donkey carts! A railroad links the towns of Kingston, Montego Bay, and Port Antonio. Kingston and Montego Bay have international airports, and there are many local airports. The national airline, Air Jamaica, has been operating since 1968.

INDUSTRY MAP

This map shows the location of Jamaica's leading industries. Bauxite is mined at several locations inland, including around Mandeville in the south. Large towns such as Kingston are centers of industry and manufacturing.

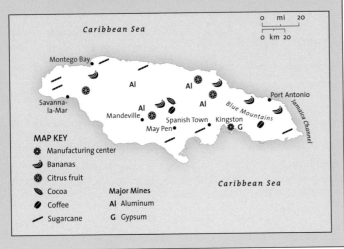

Caribbean Sea

o mi 20
o km 20

Montego Bay

Savanna-la-Mar

Mandeville
Al   Al

May Pen   Spanish Town   Kingston   G

Al   Al

Blue Mountains

Port Antonio

Jamaica Channel

Caribbean Sea

MAP KEY
- ✿ Manufacturing center
- 🍌 Bananas
- ❀ Citrus fruit
- 🍃 Cocoa
- ● Coffee
- ／ Sugarcane

Major Mines
- **Al** Aluminum
- **G** Gypsum

▼ The outskirts of Kingston are made up of poor slum districts.

Future Shocks

Jamaica's economy is doing well when compared with many Caribbean countries. In the future, natural resources such as bauxite and bananas will continue to bring prosperity. Tourism is now the island's major industry. The sunny climate and beautiful scenery will continue to draw tourists from all over the world.

However, the country does have some problems. Prices are rising fast, and there are not enough jobs for everyone. During the 1980s and 1990s Jamaica borrowed huge sums of money from the World Bank to develop industry and improve public services such as transportation, schools, and hospitals. This has left the country with huge debts.

The government now has to spend much of the income it earns from exports to pay off the interest that is due on these loans. That leaves less money to spend to help solve problems. On the other hand, the economy is boosted by funds called remittances, sent home by Jamaicans living and working abroad.

Crime is another problem. Theft is quite commonplace, especially in the cities. Crime is fueled by the large difference between the living conditions of rich and poor Jamaicans. In slums, or ghettos, tensions sometimes spill over into violence. As a result, Jamaica has one of the highest murder rates in the world. In recent years the authorities have had some success in cracking down on crime, especially in resorts, where they fear it will harm the tourist industry.

▲ Young tourists use inner tubes to float down a river in Jamaica.

New Ideas

Jamaica is aiming to develop new manufacturing and service industries, such as banking, so that it does not have to rely too heavily on tourism. Jamaican leaders are strengthening trade links with other Caribbean nations, in the hope that they can work together to compete with other regions. Whatever the future brings, Jamaicans can continue to take pride in their vibrant culture and beautiful land.

Add a Little Extra to Your Country Report!

If you are assigned to write a report about Jamaica, you'll want to include basic information about the country, of course. The Fast Facts chart on page 8 will give you a good start. The rest of the book will give you the details you need to create a full and up-to-date paper or PowerPoint presentation. But what can you do to make your report more fun than anyone else's? If you use your imagination and dig a bit deeper into some of the topics introduced in this book, you're sure to come up with information that will make your report unique!

>Flag

Perhaps you could explain the history of the Jamaican flag, and the meanings of its colors and symbol. Go to **www.crwflags.com/fotw/flags** for more information.

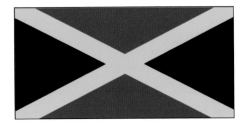

>National Anthem

How about downloading Jamaica's national anthem, and playing it for your class? At **www.nationalanthems.info** you'll find what you need, including the words to the anthem, plus sheet music for it. Simply pick "J" and then "Jamaica" from the list on the left-hand side of the screen, and you're on your way.

>Time Difference

If you want to understand the time difference between Jamaica and where you are, this Web site can help: **www.worldtimeserver.com**. Just pick "Jamaica" from the list on the left. If you called someone in Jamaica right now, would you wake them up from their sleep?

>Currency

Another Web site will convert your money into Jamaican dollars, the currency used in Jamaica. You'll want to know how much money to bring if you're ever lucky enough to travel to Jamaica: **www.xe.com/ucc**.

>Weather

Why not check the current weather in Jamaica? It's easy—go to **www.weather.com** to find out if it's sunny or cloudy, warm or cold, in Jamaica right now! Pick "World" from the headings at the top of the page. Then search for Jamaica. Click on any city.

Be sure to click on the tabs below the weather report for Sunrise/Sunset information, Weather Watch, and Business Travel Outlook, too. Scroll down the page for the 36-hour Forecast and a satellite weather map. Compare your weather to the weather in the Jamaican city you chose. Is this a good season, weather-wise, for a person to travel to Jamaica?

>Miscellaneous

Still want more information? Simply go to National Geographic's World Atlas for Young Explorers at **http://www.nationalgeographic.com/ kids-world.atlas**. It will help you find maps, photos, music, games, and other features that you can use to jazz up your report.

Glossary

Cassava a shrubby plant whose roots are often used in Jamaican cooking.

Climate the average weather of a certain place at different times of the year.

Colony a region that is ruled by a nation located somewhere else in the world. Settlers from that distant country take the land from the region's original inhabitants.

Corruption the misuse of power for private gain.

Culture a collection of beliefs, traditions, and styles that belongs to people living in a certain part of the world.

Democracy a country that is ruled by a government chosen by all its people through elections.

Dominion a country that belongs to the British Commonwealth and whose head of state is the British monarch.

Economy the system by which a country creates wealth through making and trading in products.

Ecosystem a community of living things and the environment they interact with; an ecosystem includes plants, animals, soil, water, and air.

Emigration when a person leaves his or her home country to work and live in another, usually permanently.

Flogging a severe whipping or beating that was often used to punish slaves.

Governor General someone who governs a territory on behalf of a monarch.

Habitat the environment where an animal or plant lives.

Hurricane a massive storm system that causes heavy rain and high winds and raises sea levels, often flooding low-lying land.

Karst a landscape full of gullies and caves that is formed by water dissolving soft rock, such as limestone.

Ore a naturally occurring mineral that includes deposits of valuable metals.

Plantation a large farm or estate devoted to growing one crop.

Plumage a bird's decorative feathers.

Privateer a ship given a government license to attack foreign shipping, usually in wartime.

Rural belonging to the countryside.

Smelting the process of breaking up and melting mineral ores to extract pure metals.

Species a type of organism; animals or plants in the same species look similar and can only breed successfully among themselves.

Test Match a cricket match between the world's best national teams; the matches last five days.

Trade Wind a wind that almost always blows in the same direction; trade winds were useful for sailors in the days of sailing ships.

Urban belonging to a city.

Bibliography

Barrow, Steve, and Peter Dalton. *The Rough Guide to Reggae*. London: Rough Guides, 2004.

Berry, James. *A Thief in the Village: And Other Stories of Jamaica*. London: Puffin, 1990.

Demers, John, and Eduardo Fuss. *Authentic Recipes from Jamaica*. Singapore: Periplus Editions, 2005.

Sherlock, Philip M., and Hazel Bennett. *The Story of the Jamaican People*. Jamaica: Ian

Randle Publishers, 1998.

http://www.britannica.com/ (*Encyclopaedia Britannica* online)

Further Information

NATIONAL GEOGRAPHIC Articles

Wellifoff, Alan. "Jamaica's Pirate Past." NATIONAL GEOGRAPHIC TRAVELER (October 2007): 62–63, 66.

Web sites to explore

More fast facts about Jamaica, from the CIA (Central Intelligence Agency): https://www.cia.gov/library/publications/the-world-factbook/index.html

For pictures and information about Queen Elizabeth's role in Jamaican society visit: http://www.royal.gov.uk/output/Page4923.asp

To see pictures of the island and its people, learn how to speak "Jamaican," and learn about Jamaican communities

around the world: http://www.jamaicans.com/

Find out what's on the minds of the Jamaican people from the island's oldest newspaper: http://jamaica-Gleaner.com

Visit the Jamaican Environment Trust, who protects the wildlife and natural beauty of the island: http://www.jamentrust.org

Read about the mysterious landscape of Cockpit Country, and the wildlife and plants that call it home: http://www.cockpitcountry.com

Irie FM
You can listen online to a radio station dedicated to the promotion of Jamaican culture and history: http://www.iriefm.net

Bob Marley
Visit the Bob Marley Web site

for information, interviews, and videos of some of the performances of Jamaica's most famous musician: http://web.bobmarley.com

See, Hear

The distinctive culture of this small nation has spread around the world through books, films, and, most importantly, music. You might be able to locate these:

Cool Runnings (1993)
This family film tells the story of the bobsled team that Jamaica entered at the 1988 Winter Olympics.

Tilly Bummie and Other Stories (1993)
A collection of short stories by Hazel Campbell about the lives of children living in the towns and countryside of Jamaica.

Index

Credits

Picture Credits

Front Cover – Spine: Istock ; Top: Nik Wheeler/Corbis; Low Far Left: Tim Graham/Corbis; Low Left: Howard Davies/Corbis; Low Right: Sergio Pitamitz/Zefa/Corbis; Low Far Right: Daniel Laine/Corbis.

Interior – Alamy: Tim Gartside: 18 lo; Jan Halaska: 2-3 up, 22-23; Doug Pearson: TP; Travelshots.com: 57 up; Corbis: 44 lo; Bruce Adams/Eye Ubiquitous: 55 up; James L. Amos: 53 up; Esther Anderson: 39 lo; Tony Arruza: 29 lo; Bettmann: 28 up; Bojan Brecelj: 29 up, 53 lo; Rudolph Brown: 51 lo; Jan Butchofsky-Houser 38 up; David Cummings/Eye Ubiquitous: 44 up, 48 lo; Howard Davies; 3 right, 27 up, 30 left, 43 lo, 46-47; Eye Ubiquitous: 12 up; Franz-Marc Frei: 21 up; Reinhard Eisele: 2 left, 6-7, 27 up; Alain Le Garsmeur: 56 lo; Rolf W. Hapke/Zefa: 40 up; David G. Houser: 52 left; Hulton-Deutsch: 32 lo; Daniel Laine: 45 lo; Lake County Museum: 32 up; Christian Liewig/ Transport: 41 up; Wally McNamee: 42 up; Michael Ochs Archives: 3 left, 34-35; Douglas Pearson: 5 up; Reuters: 51 up; John Riley: 13 lo; Rykcoff Collection: 31 lo; Paul Souders:10 up, 54 lo; Roberto Tedeschi: 41 lo; Werner Forman: 26 lo; Nik Wheeler: 10 lo, 54 up; Getty Images: Bridgeman Art Library: 24 lo; Bruce Dale/National Geographic: 36 lo; Jeff Greenberg/ Lonely Planet: 39 up; Hulton Archive: 33 up; NGIC: Stacy Gold: 16 lo; Robert S. Patton: 11 up; Carsten Peter 19 lo: Joel Sartore: 20 lo; NPL: Rolf Nussbaumer: 2 right, 14-15, 18 up, 21 lo; Shutterstock: Ursula: 59 up.

Text copyright © 2008 National Geographic Society
Published by the National Geographic Society.
All rights reserved. Reproduction of the whole or any part of the contents without written permission from the National Geographic Society is strictly prohibited. For information about special discounts for bulk purchases, contact National Geographic Special Sales: ngspecsales@ngs.org

For more information, please call 1-800-NGS-LINE (647-5463) or write to the following address:

NATIONAL GEOGRAPHIC SOCIETY
1145 17th Street N.W.
Washington, D.C. 20036-4688 U.S.A.

Visit us online at:
www.nationalgeographic.com/books

Library of Congress Cataloging-in-Publication Data available on request
ISBN: 978-1-4263-0300-5

Printed in the United States of America

Series design by Jim Hiscott.
The body text is set in Avenir; Knockout.
The display text is set in Matrix Script.

Front Cover—Top: Boys jump from a boat at Treasure Beach in Calabash Bay; Low Far Left: Military parade; Low Left: Coffee beans; Low Right: Scenic view of Dunn's River Falls; Low Far Right: Market in Kingston

Page 1—A statue at the Bob Marley Museum in Kingston; Icon image on spine, Contents page, and throughout: Sugarcane

Produced through the worldwide resources of the National Geographic Society

John M. Fahey, Jr., *President and Chief Executive Officer*; Gilbert M. Grosvenor, *Chairman of the Board*; Tim T. Kelly, *President, Global Media Group*; John Q. Griffin, *President, Publishing*; Nina D. Hoffman, *Executive Vice President, President of Book Publishing Group*

National Geographic Staff for this Book

Nancy Laties Feresten, *Vice President, Editor-in-Chief of Children's Books*
Bea Jackson, *Director of Design and Illustration*
Jim Hiscott, *Art Director*
Virginia Koeth, *Project Editor*
Lori Epstein, *Illustrations Editor*
Stacy Gold, Nadia Hughes, *Illustrations Research Editors*
R. Gary Colbert, *Production Director*
Lewis R. Bassford, *Production Manager*
Nicole Elliott, Rachel Faulise, *Manufacturing Managers*
Maps, Mapping Specialists, Ltd.

Brown Reference Group plc. Staff for this Book

Volume Editor: Tom Jackson
Designer: Dave Allen
Picture Manager: Clare Newman
Maps: Martin Darlison
Artwork: Darren Awuah
Index: Kay Ollerenshaw
Senior Managing Editor: Tim Cooke
Children's Publisher: Anne O'Daly
Editorial Director: Lindsey Lowe

About the Author

JEN GREEN received a doctorate from the University of Sussex, United Kingdom, in 1982. She has worked in publishing for 15 years and is now a full-time author who has written more than 150 books for children on natural history, geography, history, the environment, and other subjects.

About the Consultants

DAVID J. HOWARD is a lecturer in human geography based in the Institute of Geography at the University of Edinburgh. He has research interests in Caribbean social and urban geographies, with a particular focus on Jamaica and the Dominican Republic. He is chair of the Society for Caribbean Studies.

JOEL FRATER iis a Jamaican-born associate professor of tourism and recreation management and serves as chairperson and graduate coordinator in the Department of Recreation and Leisure Studies at State University of New York, College at Brockport. He has conducted staff development training for employees in various Caribbean resorts in customer service, leadership, recreation program planning, and multicultural understanding. His research interests are the impact of tourism, particularly in the Caribbean region, and the development of culturally sensitive training for employees in the tourism and hospitality industry.

Time Line of
Jamaican History

A.D.

ca 650 Taino Indians from the coasts of Guyana and Venezuela settle Jamaica.

800 The second wave of Taino Indians arrives in Jamaica.

1400

1494 Christopher Columbus lands at St. Ann's Bay in Jamaica.

1500

1509 The Spanish occupy Jamaica and establish the settlements of Sevilla la Nueva and Spanish Town.

1517 Spanish settlers import the first African slaves to work in the sugarcane fields.

ca 1520 Jamaica's last Taino Indians die due to exposure to European diseases.

1600

1655 British forces capture Spanish Town.

1664 400 British planters move from Barbados to Jamaica to develop its sugar economy.

1670 By the terms of the Treaty of Madrid Spain must hand control of Jamaica to Britain.

1690 The First Maroon War begins when slaves rebel in Clarendon, setting fire to plantations and killing livestock.

1692 An earthquake devastates Port Royal, half of which sinks underwater.

1693 The new city of Kingston becomes the center of Jamaican power.

1700

1728 Sir Nicholas Lawes introduces coffee to Jamaica from the French West Indies.

1738 British governors sign a peace treaty with Cudjoe, a Maroon leader from Cockpit Country, to end the First Maroon War. The Maroons agree to stop attacking British settlements in return for the right to govern themselves and an area of land.

1760 Tackey, a slave, starts a slave rebellion in Port Maria that spreads throughout the island and kills 400 slaves and 60 white Jamaicans.

1782 Three-Fingered Jack leads a slave rebellion in St. Mary's.

1795 The Second Maroon War begins in Trelawny Parish when Maroons protesting their mistreatment are taken prisoner by the British. To stop the revolt, the British bring in dogs to hunt escaped slaves and deport 600 Maroons to Nova Scotia and Sierra Leone.

1800

1808 Britain abolishes the slave trade and importation of slaves to Jamaica becomes illegal.

1838 Slavery is abolished in Jamaica; all slaves are freed.

1865 The government in Jamaica puts down the Morant Bay rebellion, and executes two innocent men. The British government forces the local legislature to give up its powers and Jamaica becomes a British crown colony.